Mary —
 I hope to meet you someday..
is a good guy.

 Yours truly,

 Jim H.

Words To Breathe By

James Richard Hansen

authorHOUSE

AuthorHouse™
1663 Liberty Drive
Bloomington, IN 47403
www.authorhouse.com
Phone: 833-262-8899

© 2020 James Richard Hansen. All rights reserved.

No part of this book may be reproduced, stored in a retrieval system, or transmitted by any means without the written permission of the author.

Published by AuthorHouse 06/05/2020

ISBN: 978-1-7283-6381-3 (sc)
ISBN: 978-1-7283-6380-6 (e)

Library of Congress Control Number: 2020910418

Print information available on the last page.

Any people depicted in stock imagery provided by Getty Images are models, and such images are being used for illustrative purposes only.
Certain stock imagery © Getty Images.

This book is printed on acid-free paper.

Because of the dynamic nature of the Internet, any web addresses or links contained in this book may have changed since publication and may no longer be valid. The views expressed in this work are solely those of the author and do not necessarily reflect the views of the publisher, and the publisher hereby disclaims any responsibility for them.

For my wife Kristen and all my family and friends
who have supported me through the years

In memory of my parents Paul G. and Darlene R. Hansen

Contents

Enraptured 1
The Arriving Night 2
Trees 3
Clouds Of Mist 4
A Fantasy Of White 5
Prelude 6
Stars 7
Rain 8
River Of Peace 9
Orchids 10
Glorious Gifts 11
Caring 13
Land And Sky 14
The Road To Happiness 15
Morning Magic 16
Solitude 17
Songs 18
Touch Of The Moon 19
Poetry 20
Father 21
Taking Away The Chill 22
Skyscape 23

Revival 24
A Cool, Damp Coat 25
Phantasmagoria 26
Healer 27
Grandeur 28
Questions And Answers 29
Sunfall 30
Maya 31

Love Poems For Kristen

Anticipation 35
Oasis 36
Cloud Nine 37
Jewel Of The Pacific 38
Where Are You From? 39
More Than Enough 40
Your Brilliant Blues 41
Popularity 42
Never 43
Sapphire 44
Returning Home 45
Hope 46
Reflections 47
Relief 48
Our Time 49
Reasons 50
Search 51
Golden Music 52
You 53
Soaring 54

Enraptured

As the early orange sun
begins to take back the sky,
and the stars become invisible,
I relish the fresh morning air
and the calm, cool breeze
that blows through my hair
and fills my lungs.
In a moment,
I become enraptured with the dawn
after a tempest of trouble
the night before.
Nightmares turn to gold,
and I am young again.

The Arriving Night

The long day wanes,
and the stunning blue sky fades
in the midst of pristine white clouds.
The blinding fall of the sun
burns red near the horizon.
Soon, I feel the arriving night
and welcome the stars and moon
with their pearly glow and cryptic aura.
They pull me into their world.
I fly and float in the blackness of space
as the night lights illuminate
the wonder of the universe,
even in the midst of a void.

Trees

As I wander down the path
wondering about my life path,
I am struck by the immensity of the sequoias
and the many wonders they represent;
grand old men, advanced in years
and showing the effects of age,
but strong from a lifetime of nourishment and struggle.
I hope to be like them someday—
having learned about life,
standing strong and straight and tall,
enduring almost anything,
and giving shelter to those around me.

Clouds Of Mist

Falling from the cliff,
the cataract billows clouds of mist
as it plunges to the valley floor.
I am close enough
to feel the spray on my face and arms
bringing me to life.
I eat my lunch in the midst of the mist.

After finishing,
I leave the cliff, cataract, and mist
and return to civilization,
knowing that soon
I will visit the park again
to experience what I,
as a city dweller, need.

A Fantasy Of White

The falling, blowing snow
drifts into no shape I know,
but seems to follow a pattern
like snowflakes themselves.
I drift in a fantasy of white
fueled by pristine memories.
I haven't seen real snow
in over a decade—
only pictures.
But memories abound
with days of play
in piles of white
after a big storm.

Prelude

Autumn sun gleams off the sea
as it sets in my dusky eyes.
I float in the heavens with cirrus clouds,
their protean essence educed by Promethean wind.

Scarlet and orange parade across the clouds
as they frame the sun's passage
to darkness.

Prelude to night ends.
Night unfolds.

Stars

The glorious night—
its splendor of galactic lights
taking away my breath—
leads me through my imagination,
the stars a lucent guide
illuminating the infinitude of the universe.

Rain

Morning, in its abundant riches,
greets me with the beauty of rain.
The pain I experience daily
does not dampen the joy of morning,
its spirit melding with mine.
When I stand in the rain
on a rare day without sunshine,
I feel its cleansing power
dripping down my skin,
purging the emotional debris
of life's daily battles.

River Of Peace

My source of peace
is a river of cool, fresh water,
a river I can drink from,
a river that soothes my skin
and calms my spirit.
These gifts are only for those
who truly search for them.

River of peace within,
help me find my way
in this tumultuous world.

Orchids

Like big, bizarre faces,
they stare at me with two huge eyes,
each covering an entire side of the face.
The mouth is from "Alien,"
ready to gobble the life out of me.
The top is like a bishop's miter
rising between the two gargantuan eyes.
Solid white except for a little
orange, yellow, and green in the mouth,
each is a beautiful monster,
coming closer every day.

Glorious Gifts

I

Vermilion clouds hide the sun,
but not its resplendence,
as the blazing ball slides into the sea.
Evening fades, and the night sky
comes alive with scintillating stars
and the silvery glow of the moon.

II

I reminisce about the hundreds of sunsets
I've seen since moving to southern California—
hues I'd never seen in a sunset,
dazzling varieties and mixtures of cloud shapes,
miraculous psychedelic effects on the Pacific—
often followed by a voyage beyond this world
as the moon, in one of its many magical phases,
joined with countless stars for a light show.

III

I try not to dwell on the darkness in life,
but bask in the splendor of home.
I want to die here in paradise.
As that time comes closer,
I hope to build a life worthy
of the glory I witness every day and night.

Caring

For Victoria

In the front yard of our condo,
a Monarch butterfly
darts around our Mexican milkweed.
Beautiful, fragile, but strong in its own way,
its transformation
from caterpillar to chrysalis to masterpiece
was unseen and mysterious,
but perfect.
I shed a tear of pain
thinking it must have suffered,
but a tear of joy
watching it live as a work of art.
Were it human,
I would want it to shed a tear for me,
as you did.

Land And Sky

Sounds of the air
rushing through the trees
The feel of the breeze
blowing through my hair
The scent of spring flowers
filling my mind and heart
Sunlight warming my body
The beauty of land and sky
warming my day.

The Road To Happiness

I was charting my course by the stars,
but they fell from the sky
in an avalanche of light.
I was crushed by the immensity
and blinded by the intensity.

I search for something to believe.
I need something to believe.
No one has shown me
the road to happiness.
How will I find my way?

Morning Magic

I feel myself waking
as my body stirs
and my mind returns from its journey.
Through our glass door,
in the half-light of dawn,
I see the miracle of nature coming to life.
The early morning glow
lights iridescent jewels of dew.
Glorious roses, camellias, and daffodils
light my eyes.
Puffy white clouds
frame the fronds and trunks of palm trees
against the pale sky.
My day has begun with an electric charge.

Solitude

A cataract crashes onto boulders a short distance away.
Standing back from the bank, I am protected by pines
from most of the moisture billowing in the breeze.
I am far from the main trails and farther from the parking lots
where groups of tourists gather. I relish my isolation.

Dusk approaches, so I head back to my car
with only wildlife for company.
Solitude is delicious, as Einstein said.
I need it to survive.

But as I walk out of the wilderness,
I begin to hear sounds of tourists
talking and laughing, the joy palpable.
Solitude isn't everything.

Songs

The day was long,
but so was the night.
I slept and laughed,
cried and tossed.
I sang a serenade
to the goddess of the night
as I gazed at the full moon.
I sang an aubade
to the sun god
as dawn greeted my tears.

Touch Of The Moon

The huge orb casts its spell
as I stroll in the icy night.
I feel its touch as I reflect
on the troubles and triumphs of my day.
As I bathe in the silvery glow,
wisps of white slowly veil the moon,
then dense clouds hide it completely.
Still, I see its light and feel its pull
as I walk down the dark street
toward my home and sleep.

Poetry

The music of words
resounding in all the senses,
the sweet fragrance of sound,
the lustrous picturesque hues,
the delicate but powerful touch
of imagination and ideas,
all transcending time and space
and penetrating body and mind,
renewing the Self.

Father

A day of nights,
a night of nightmares.
I still cry for my father,
for our wonderful but flawed relationship,
for the life song we sang together.
I stopped singing the day he died.

But now I sing a new song.
Life is new, fueled by my father within me.

Taking Away The Chill

In our garden, the flowers and leaves
glitter in their fresh coat of spring rain,
taking away my pain.
The beauty of the natural world
heals my wounds
from the uglier parts of life.

Sunshine on my face and neck
takes away the chill of the rainy day.

Skyscape

I sit on a cloud, and dream.
But surrounding clouds, sun, and wind
capture my awareness
and bring me back to reality.
The magnificent scene
transcends even my dreams.

Revival

The sun sinks like my heart.
It sets in a flurry of scarlet and orange,
with cirrus clouds adding
to the mercurial mix.
The rising moon sparks my recovery,
and a little sparkle comes back to my eyes.
I am alive again.

A Cool, Damp Coat

Rain spatters our patio and my body
as I lie on a lounge chair.
My skin feels the cool, damp coat
of refreshment; the spotted cement
is soon completely wet.
I breathe deeply, filling my lungs
with air purged of smog and dust.
As the sun breaks through clouds
near the horizon, the rain abates,
and the wind reorders the sky to reveal
the pale moon growing brighter.
The sun disappears.

Phantasmagoria

As I ponder the protean clouds,
they transform into shapes
reflecting my inner life.
The clouds become
a phantasmagoria
of unfamiliar parts
of my psyche.
I am transfixed,
living the show
in all its joy and dread.

Healer

For Lisa

As you have said,
we are two dolphins on parallel paths.
But dolphins don't have hands.

Your soothing touch and dulcet voice,
with your soft, salutary spirit,
comfort and relieve

and push the limits
of the healing arts.

Two wounded healers
helping each other grow.

Grandeur

I stand in a large open area
surrounded by pines.
Night abounds with luminous starlight,
the Milky Way visible in clear mountain air.
The moon lends power
to the scene through its absence.
I hear crickets, wolves, and frogs,
and trees rustling in the wind.
Night's chill adds to the thrill.

Questions And Answers

In daylight, I see clearly.
I need no artificial aids.
But when night arrives,
the mystery begins,
and I stumble and lose my way.

When daylight returns,
I have answers,
though I never knew
there were questions
until I lost myself in the night.

Sunfall

The blinding, falling disc spreads its wings across the horizon
as I gaze at the picturesque clouds
and devour the brilliant orange and scarlet sky.
As the sun drops and disappears,
I peel my eyes from the fading grandeur
and close them to outer and inner darkness.

Maya

She was a wonder during her seventeen years,
leaping unreal heights
and gracefully running through our condo
and around the corners at full speed.

She was small—
seven pounds at her heaviest—
with beautiful silky black fur
and some white.

She loved to go outside
on our front and back patios
to eat grass,
drink the rain water she loved,
and soak up the sun
while she napped.

When we petted her,
she looked at us
with love.

She was the sweetest spirit
I've ever known,
animal or human.
Everyone who met her
said how sweet and good she was,
either with their words or their eyes.

When the vets discovered her cancer,
it was too advanced for effective treatment.

She weighed about three pounds.

I don't think she suffered much,
but cats hide pain well.
At the end, she did suffer,
so we did the merciful thing.

Love Poems For Kristen

Anticipation

You walked toward me
in the dim light of the train station.
Your walk was slow, natural,
and subtly sexy.
It was the first time I'd seen you
since we met a month before,
hundreds of miles away.
After thirty emails, twenty poems,
and five two-hour phone calls,
we decided we had to be
together.
So I came down on the train.
And as you slowly moved
toward me, I was eager for
the first hug,
the first kiss.
It would be our first night
together.

Oasis

When I see roses in bloom,
or sense the fragrance of lilacs in fresh air,
or witness the wonder of lavender in a spring shower,
I think of you.
You are an array of precious stones in a pristine stream,
a panoply of stunning sights and soothing sounds
in a world of cold steel and burning oil.
You are my oasis.
When I am with you,
I remember the good in the world.

You rescued me.
I live among the treasures of your garden
and experience your inner gold.
You opened the gates of paradise.

Cloud Nine

In a warm, tranquil sky,
I meet my lover on a cloud
for a secret rendezvous.
The terrestrial world is too base,
too banal to meet there.

She is lounging
in sunlight, stretched
across a silky white bed.
Our celestial work of art
has just begun.

Jewel Of The Pacific

the waters of your blue eyes

caress the shore of my soul.

I bask in the sun of your love,

rich in the warmth you bring.

Another year of heaven.

Your gift.

Where Are You From?

In your soul's light,
I stop wasting time making war
and look for peace,
helped by your endless reserve.
What cross produced this treasure
for the world?
Your soul was refined
in the crucible of life,
but born in a better place.

More Than Enough

You are a diamond,
but soft.
You are redolent of roses,
but without thorns.
I want to touch you
in the pure morning light.
I want to love you like God.
I hope the love of a mere mortal is enough.
Being loved by you is ecstasy.

Your Brilliant Blues

The day we met,
I saw a bright light in your eyes
and saw the light.
With your brilliant blues,
you revealed yourself
and captured me instantly.
But I'm not, and never was,
a prisoner.
I have never felt so free.
And with your love for me,
I have flourished
in your garden of healing magic.

Popularity

The sun beamed when he told me you are a bright star.
The moon glowed when she told me you are romantic.
I spoke with a saint, who blessed you for being loving and patient.
A flamingo proclaimed your beauty to its entire flock.
Of course, I already knew about these qualities and many more.
But I'm glad they have made you famous.

Never

Never will the darkness in life
extinguish the glow of our love.
Never will the evil of the world
destroy our goodness.
Never will our passion be cooled
by the coldness of others.

In the time we have been together,
our togetherness has become unity.
Yet we remain separate and unique.

Sapphire

I found you in God's jewelry store,
a perfectly polished sapphire
in a diamond setting.
The price was beyond my means.
But God said I could have you
as long as I promised
to love and care for you faithfully.
I told God I would be more devoted
than humanly possible.

Now, you are more valuable than ever.
And with your help,
I have polished myself a little.

Returning Home

Into the distance I ride
on a horse of the imagination.
I travel to strange, distant lands
in search of myself.
I meet people of all types
and experience exotic cultures
and stunning sights.
But my search is futile.

I return home and find you
waiting to welcome me
and tell me you love me.
Here with you
is where I will find myself.

Hope

Dust had settled on my dreams.
But that was fourteen years ago,
when hope had all but flown.
I persevered, then you appeared.

My persistence was rewarded
thousands of times in you.
My hope became reality in you.
You are angelic, pristine.

Our life together blossomed
into a paradise
I had never conceived.
And the dust has disappeared.

Reflections

As we reflect on our lives in Shangri-la,
our mirror gleams in our eyes,
showing our past and present
and illuminating our future with timeless beauty.
The mirror brings into focus our wondrous reality
in the cascade of love that drowns us in each other.

Relief

Instead of stars giving rise to the sun,
the moon sets to darkness.
I stroll on my street,
hoping for a breakthrough
to relieve my pain.

There is no relief, no light.
But as I near home,
I see you
standing in the porch light
welcoming me.

Our Time

In our life together,
the sun has given us miracles;
we have been led to each other
by the moon;
the stars have stunned us
and made us aware;
the universe has welcomed us
into the realm of joy.

In the time we spend together,
nothing surpasses
the times we say, "I love you."

Reasons

I plunge into warm water,
feeling it soothe my skin,
and my anger,
as I dive deeper.
I can no longer recall
the precise reason for my mood.
But I know it won't weaken our bond.
Our ties are too strong.

You walk to poolside
as I climb out.
We hug and kiss,
our unity stronger than ever.

Search

Instead of hurting forever,
instead of longing forever,
instead of dreaming forever,
I found you.

The end of my search
was the beginning of my life.

Golden Music

The air breathes you, as I do.
The sun soaks up your glow,
and the wind blows
with the strength of your spirit.
Your heart is golden music,
in step with my body,
in tune with my heart.
Our song, born of our love
and cradled in the universe,
will grow until it embraces
all the music of our lives.

You

Your eyes ignite my heart.
Your hair is blond sunshine,
your silken skin covered with dew.
Your body is a temple;
I worship at the altar.
Our time together is one,
our love timeless.
May it last until the end of time.

Soaring

For our marriage

When we stroll in sunlight,
its brilliance is surpassed
only by the resplendence of our love.
When we walk under the moon,
its glow creates a mood
we need no help creating.
Our warmth reaches to the moon,
creating a midnight sun
that overcomes any darkness in our lives.
We are filled with love
we never knew we could feel,
and passion that leaves us
breathless.
We breathe each other
and soar to the peak
of ecstasy and fulfillment.
Our bond will last forever,
not because we promise,
but because no power
could tear us apart.
It is written in our hearts.

Printed in the USA
CPSIA information can be obtained
at www.ICGtesting.com
JSHW080749171123
51918JS00004B/31